Best Easy Day Hikes
Yosemite National Park

A **FALCON** GUIDE®

Best Easy Day Hikes Series

Best Easy Day Hikes
Yosemite National
Park

Second Edition

Suzanne Swedo

FALCON GUIDE®

GUILFORD, CONNECTICUT
HELENA, MONTANA

AN IMPRINT OF THE GLOBE PEQUOT PRESS

For Mom

Help Us Keep This Guide Up to Date

Every effort has been made by the author and editors to make this guide as accurate and useful as possible. However, many things can change after a guide is published—trails are rerouted, regulations change, facilities come under new management, etc.

We would love to hear from you concerning your experiences with this guide and how you feel it could be improved and kept up to date. While we may not be able to respond to all comments and suggestions, we'll take them to heart and we'll also make certain to share them with the author. Please send your comments and suggestions to the following address:

> The Globe Pequot Press
> Reader Response/Editorial Department
> P.O. Box 480
> Guilford, CT 06437

Or you may e-mail us at:

> editorial@GlobePequot.com

Thanks for your input, and happy trails!

Contents

Yosemite National Park

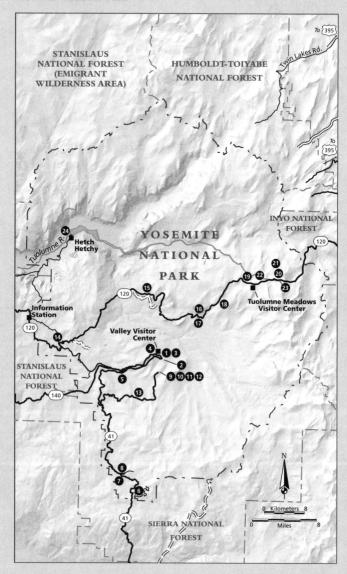

Tuolumne Meadows Trails

Acknowledgments

Thanks to the National Park Service, especially Ranger Mark Fincher, whose suggestions and advice were invaluable. Thanks also to the personnel and volunteers of the Yosemite Association.

Ranking the Hikes

The following list ranks the hikes in this book from easiest to hardest.

Easiest

9   Glacier Point
4   Lower Yosemite Fall
5   Bridalveil Fall
3   Mirror Lake
1   East Valley Floor
17 Olmstead Point Nature Trail
23 Lyell Fork
8   Chilnualna Falls
7   Wawona Meadow
6   Mariposa Grove
22 Soda Springs and Parsons Lodge
19 Pothole Dome
13 McGurk Meadow
2   Happy Isles to Vernal Fall
18 Tenaya Lake
15 Lukens Lake
16 May Lake
14 Tuolumne Grove
12 Taft Point and the Fissures
20 Dog Lake
21 Lembert Dome
24 Wapama Falls
11 Sentinel Dome
10 Illilouette Fall

Hardest

Introduction

This book is for a great many of the nearly four million visitors to Yosemite each year who have a limited amount of time to spend, but want to sample some of the best features of the park on foot. Yosemite's borders encompass almost 1,200 square miles in east-central California, though the majority of tourists congregate in Yosemite Valley and miss much of the spectacular wild country beyond. The hikes described here are scattered throughout the entire park. All are accessible by paved roads and none is difficult to find.

The hikes vary in length, but none is longer than 5 miles. The shorter hikes are not necessarily the easier ones. Because this is rugged country with few level places, most hikes do involve a little elevation gain and loss. Use the list of hikes ranked in order of difficulty to make your choice. All are on easy-to-follow, clearly marked trails.

Zero Impact

The trails that weave through Yosemite National Park are heavily used and take a real beating. Because of their proximity to pollution and dense population, we—as trail users and advocates—must be vigilant to make sure our passing leaves no lasting mark. If we all left our mark on the landscape, the parks and wildlands eventually would be destroyed.

These trails can accommodate plenty of human travel if everybody treats them with respect. Just a few thoughtless, badly mannered, or uninformed visitors can ruin them for everyone who follows. The book *Leave No Trace* (www.falcon.com) is a valuable resource for learning more about these principles.

The Falcon Zero-Impact Principles

- Leave with everything you brought with you.
- Leave no sign of your visit.
- Leave the landscape as you found it.

Litter is the scourge of all trails. It is unsightly, polluting, and potentially dangerous to wildlife. Pack out all your own trash, including biodegradable items like orange peels. You should also pack out garbage left trailside by other hikers. Store a plastic bag in your pack to use for trash removal.

Don't approach or feed any wild creatures—the ground squirrel eyeing your snack food is best able to survive if it remains self-reliant, since it is not likely to find cookies along the trail when winter comes.

Never pick flowers or gather plants or insects. So many people visit these trails that the cumulative effect of individual impacts can be great.

Stay on established trails. Shortcutting and cutting switchbacks promote erosion. Select durable surfaces, like rocks, logs, or sandy areas, for resting spots. Be courteous by not making loud noises while hiking.

Some of the trails described in this guide also are used by horseback riders. Acquaint yourself with proper trail etiquette and be courteous. Consider volunteering time to trail maintenance projects, giving something back to the parks and trails you enjoy.

If possible, use outhouses at trailheads or along the trail. If not, pack in a lightweight trowel to use to bury your waste 6 to 8 inches deep. Pack out used toilet paper in a plastic bag. Make sure you relieve yourself at least 300 feet away from any surface water or boggy spot and off any established trail.

Remember to abide by the golden rule of backcountry travel: If you pack it in, pack it out! Keep your impact to a minimum by taking only pictures and leaving only footprints.

Practice these principles of zero impact—put your ear to the ground and listen carefully. Thousands of people coming behind you are thankful for your courtesy and good sense.

Play It Safe

Generally, hiking in Yosemite National Park is safe and fun. Though there are no guarantees, there is much you can do to help ensure each outing is a safe and enjoyable one. Below you'll find an abbreviated list of hiking dos and don'ts, but by no means should this list be considered comprehensive. You are strongly encouraged to verse yourself in the art of backcountry travel.

Know the basics of first aid, including how to treat bleeding, bites and stings, and fractures, strains, or sprains. Few of the hikes are so remote that help can't be reached within a short time, but you'd be wise to carry and know how to use simple supplies, such as over-the-counter pain relievers, bandages, and ointments. Pack a first-aid kit on each excursion.

The sun can be unrelenting in the Sierra Nevada; carry a sunscreen with a minimum 15 SPF and apply it often. The weather also can change abruptly in any season. Carry clothing items to protect you from sudden and dramatic temperature changes and/or rain and snow. Remember, summer thunderstorms aren't uncommon in the mountains and may bring dangers such as lightning, hail, and high winds.

The mountains are home to a variety of wildlife, from squirrels to mountain lions. Squirrels can be hosts to disease, and mountain lions may attack if prompted by hunger. Rattlesnakes may be found on a few of these hikes, particularly from early spring to midfall. Watch where you put your hands and feet. If given a chance, most rattlesnakes will try to avoid a confrontation.

The same flora and fauna that make hiking such a relief from the daily grind also possess potential hazards for unwary hikers. Know how to identify poison oak, which can be bothersome at lower elevations.

Ticks are another pest to be avoided. They hang in the brush waiting to drop on warm-blooded animals (people included). Check for ticks and remove any before they have a chance to bite.

It is wise to bring more drinking water than you think you'll need. Generally, bring thirty-two ounces for each hour of hiking per person. Most free-flowing water should be considered unsafe to drink if untreated.

You'll enjoy each of these hikes—whether short and easy or long and strenuous—much more if you wear good socks and appropriate footwear.

Carry a comfortable day pack containing snacks and/or lunch, and extra clothing. Maps are not necessary, but they are fun to have along. You also can pack other items to increase your enjoyment of the hike, like a camera, a manual to help identify plants and wildflowers, and binoculars.

Bears

Yosemite's black bears pose little threat to hikers, but they do break into parked vehicles they suspect might contain food. Many cars are damaged by bears each year. The bears' sense of smell is so acute they can detect a single wrapped and sealed candy bar in your trunk and may dismantle your car to get it. They are very intelligent; they know food comes in cans, ice chests, and paper and plastic bags, and they will break in to check out any of these items even if they are empty. Keep all ice chests and items that might appear to contain food hidden, and stow *all* food, fresh or freeze-dried, wrapped or unwrapped, in the bear-proof boxes provided at trailheads.

Shuttle Buses

Yosemite operates free shuttle buses between trailheads and main points of interest. During the summer season between 7:00 A.M. and 10:00 P.M., the buses run every ten minutes in Yosemite Valley, every hour in Tuolumne Meadows, and every twenty minutes in the Wawona area. The *Yosemite Guide* newspaper, given to visitors at each park entrance, has a map of bus routes and a schedule for buses in Yosemite Valley. You can pick up a Tuolumne Meadows schedule at the visitor center in Tuolumne Meadows. The shuttles are a convenient, low-impact way to enjoy Yosemite. Trailhead parking is sometimes limited, and bears breaking into cars at trailheads is a concern. There is no gasoline available in Yosemite Valley.

Map Legend

⌣	Bridge
▲	Campground
•—•	Gate
🚶	Horse Trail
▬	Lodging
▲	Mountain/Peak
▣	Overlook/Viewpoint
🅿	Parking
)(	Pass
🎪	Picnic
■	Point of Interest
⬛	Ranger Station
⌐	Spring
🥾	Trailhead
+	UTM grid tick
∦	Waterfall
⑳ 395	U.S. Highway
⑳ 120	State Highway
▬▬	U.S. Highway
——	Other Paved Road
═══	Gravel Road
═══	Unimproved Road
------	Trail
▬▬▬	Highlighted Route
—·—·—	Intermittent River/Lake
——	River/Creek
▬	Lake/Large River
⸖ ⸖	Marsh/Swamp
— - -	Park Boundary

Trails in Yosemite Valley

1 East Valley Floor

Type of hike: Loop.
Total distance: 2.6 miles.
Elevation gain: None.
Topo map: USGS Half Dome.
Starting point: Curry Village.

Best time to go: All year.
Facilities: Food, supplies, phones, water, and restrooms are available at Curry Village.

Finding the trailhead: Board the Yosemite Valley shuttle bus from anywhere in the Valley and get off at stop 13, Curry Village, or leave your car in the big parking lot at Curry Village at the southeast end of the valley.

The Hike

From the raised patio area in front of the bustling Curry Village snack bar/grocery/bike rental complex, look beyond the enormous parking lot on your left (north) to towering North Dome and the Royal Arches, serene and indifferent to the hubbub below. Follow the paved footpath eastward, past a line of tent cabins fronted by a row of large, brown, steel bear-proof boxes for nighttime storage of food, toothpaste, and other aromatic bear-tempting articles. If you set out before 9:00 A.M., a good idea in midsummer when valley temperatures climb into the eighties, you are likely to pass a row of bleary-eyed tent cabin guests brushing their teeth and generally preparing for the day.

About 100 yards beyond the tent cabins and the toothbrush brigade, a driveway turns right (south) into a parking

East Valley Floor

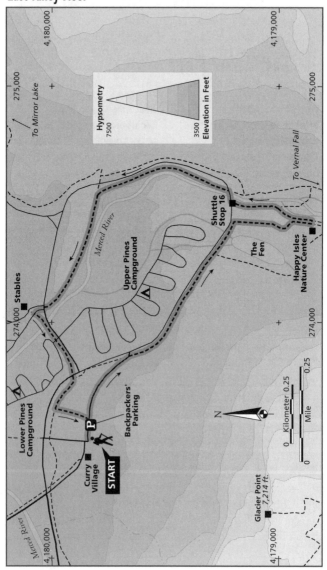

lot for backpackers. Go into the lot, turn left, and walk to its southeast end. Take the unmarked but wide and obvious trail into the shady ponderosa pine and incense cedar forest. Pass a little A-frame structure used for ranger and naturalist talks, and at 0.9 mile reach a swampy area known as The Fen. Here, a boardwalk runs through a lush growth of water-loving horsetails, sedges, and fragrant mints. An interpretive panel explains what lives in soggy places like The Fen. The trail crosses a paved path at 1.0 mile, just before it meets the Merced River. To the right (south) is the Happy Isles Nature Center, with wonderful exhibits and books inside. Behind the building you can see the rubble and smashed trees left by the 1996 rockslide that killed a hiker.

From the nature center backtrack to the north (downstream) and follow the riverside path to the shuttle bus road (stop 16) at 1.1 miles. There are restrooms and a snack bar here.

This hike crosses the road and continues downstream along the north bank of the Merced, but take a minute to follow the road onto the Happy Isles Bridge for views of the river, which rushes toward the bridge in noisy white-water rapids, then emerges from the other side more quietly and sedately. The view of North Dome on the downstream side is a photographer's favorite.

Once you have crossed the road, you leave the crowds behind and follow a path through incense cedars and pines, streamside alders, and dogwoods. Big, showy white azaleas perfume the air in May and June. The river changes charac-ter at every turn, sometimes gurgling busily, sometimes green and placid, occasionally splitting to flow around wooded islands. This section of the trail is shared by horses and mules because it connects the stables to the John Muir

Trail. Remember to step off the trail to let the horses pass; pack animals always have the right of way.

At 2.0 miles the stable area appears across the road on the right (north), and simultaneously Upper Yosemite Fall comes into view. Turn left (west), and follow the road over the Clark Bridge, which spans the Merced. Pass between the entrances to Upper and Lower Pines Campgrounds. A sign directs you to Curry Village; just beyond, you will spot the tent cabins for the employees of the village. The Curry Village parking lot and the end of the hike lie to the right (west).

Miles and Directions

0.0   Trailhead.
0.1   Reach the backpackers' parking lot.
0.9   Pass The Fen.
1.0   Reach the Happy Isles Nature Center.
1.1   Cross the Happy Isles Bridge on the shuttle bus road.
2.0   Pass the stables.
2.6   Curry Village.

2 Happy Isles to Vernal Fall

Type of hike: Out-and-back.
Total distance: 1.6 miles.
Elevation gain: 400 feet.
Topo map: USGS Half Dome.
Starting point: Happy Isles.

Best time to go: Spring, summer, or fall.
Facilities: A snack bar, water, toilets, and telephones are available at Happy Isles.

Finding the trailhead: Board the Yosemite Valley shuttle bus at any stop in the Valley and get off at stop 16, Happy Isles. Curry Village has parking nearest the trailhead.

The Hike

This may be the finest hike in Yosemite Valley. The Merced River first plunges over the steps of the Giant Staircase as Nevada Fall, then as Vernal Fall, before it slows to sweeping meanders over the flat floor of Yosemite Valley. If time permits, you can hike or drive up to Glacier Point for a spectacular overhead view of the Giant Staircase.

The trail begins at Happy Isles, site of the notorious rockfall of July 1996. Cross the Happy Isles Bridge and turn right (south) along the east shore of the Merced River. A huge sign marks the beginning of the John Muir Trail, showing mileage to various points along the way to the trail's end at Mount Whitney, 211 miles to the south.

The first part of this trail was paved at one time, but because the asphalt has washed away in places over the years, it's sometimes rough and rocky. Don't expect a true wilderness here. This is a popular spot for good reasons: The view is spectacular, and this trail is probably the most heavily used route out of the valley to the high country.

Happy Isles to Vernal Fall

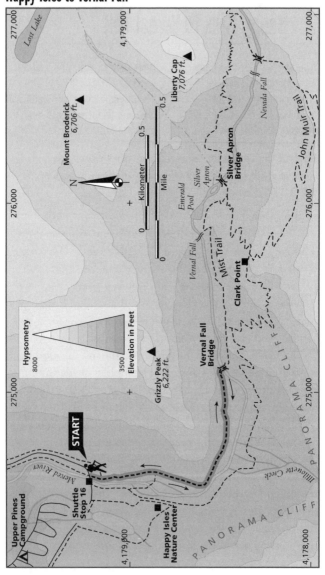

The trail climbs through black oak and pine forest among enormous lichen-draped boulders along the east bank of the Merced. A little spring trickles out of the rocks about 100 yards up on your left (east). Don't drink the water without purifying it. The trail steepens gradually as you climb, but you will want to stop frequently anyway to enjoy the roaring river through openings in the trees.

After about 0.5 mile look across the Merced to your right (south). Tucked back up in Illilouette Gorge, the Illilouette Fall pours 370 feet down the Panorama Cliff to meet the Merced River. If you stop now and then to glance behind you, you will find that Upper Yosemite Fall is visible, too.

The trail descends to the bridge at 0.8 mile, where dozens of visitors will be taking photos or staring in open-mouthed wonder at 317-foot Vernal Fall. There are restrooms nearby, a water fountain, and dozens of freeloading Steller's jays and ground squirrels. For their health and your safety, do not feed them. When you are ready, return the way you came.

Miles and Directions

0.0   Happy Isles Trailhead.
0.5   Views open to Illilouette Fall.
0.8   Reach Vernal Fall Bridge.
1.6   Happy Isles.

3 Mirror Lake

Type of hike: Out-and-back.
Total distance: 2.0 miles.
Elevation gain: 100 feet.
Topo map: USGS Half Dome.
Starting point: Shuttle bus stop 17 at Mirror Lake.
Best time to go: The trail is accessible year-round, but it is finest in May and June, when the dogwoods are blooming and the water level is high enough for Half Dome to cast the reflection that gives the lake its name.
Facilities: There are restrooms at the trailhead, but no running water.

Finding the trailhead: Board the Yosemite Valley shuttle bus at any stop in the Valley and get off at stop 17, Mirror Lake. Curry Village has parking nearest the trailhead.

The Hike

Mirror Lake was created when a rockslide dammed up a section of Tenaya Creek, which promptly went to work to reclaim its original course. Every spring the creek washes tons of silt down the canyon to refill the lake basin, extending fingers of earth out into the water. This in turn invites colonization by water-loving plants such as sedges and willows, which soon come alive with the songs of red-winged blackbirds.

Mirror Lake is well on its way to becoming Mirror Meadow. Eventually, as the basin fills in and dries out, the area will become a conifer forest with Tenaya Creek running through it—perhaps leaving the canyon as though Mirror Lake had never been—at least until the next rockslide. For years the National Park Service periodically dredged the lake, slowing the natural succession from lake to forest in

Mirror Lake

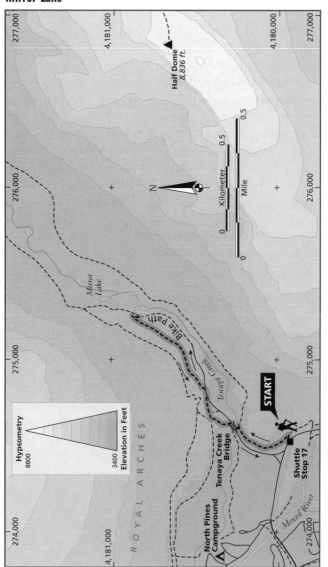

order to preserve the popular reflection, but the practice was eventually discontinued. Interpretive exhibits along the trail help visitors appreciate the way the natural world continuously transforms itself.

From the shuttle bus stop, the sign for Mirror Lake points you along the paved road (no longer used by vehicles except for bicycles), across the Tenaya Creek Bridge, and past an interpretive panel on the right (east) detailing the Yosemite flood of January 1997. That year an unseasonable thaw sent runoff from a wetter-than-normal snowpack raging through the valley, gouging out the streambed and raising the water level as much as 20 feet above normal. The flood washed out roads, bridges, campgrounds, and housing and temporarily closed down the park. Beyond this panel you can leave the road and follow a signed footpath on the left (northwest) or continue on the road, which is the more scenic route since it follows the creek.

Both road and trail rise slightly, passing through a quiet forest of ponderosa pine, white fir, Douglas fir, incense cedar, and dogwood. At 1.0 mile the forest opens to reveal tranquil Mirror Lake, reflecting Half Dome above. Mount Watkins provides the backdrop to the north. There are sandy beaches along the lakeshore for picnics and wading. Return the way you came.

Miles and Directions

- **0.0**   Trailhead.
- **1.0**   Reach Mirror Lake.
- **2.0**   Trailhead.

4 Lower Yosemite Fall

Type of hike: Loop.
Total distance: 0.6 mile.
Elevation gain: Minimal.
Topo maps: USGS Half Dome and Yosemite Falls.
Starting point: Shuttle bus stop 7 at the Yosemite Falls parking lot.

Best time to go: November to mid-August.
Facilities: There are pit toilets at the trailhead; food and supplies are available at nearby Yosemite Lodge.

Finding the trailhead: Ride the shuttle bus from any one of the nineteen stops around the Valley.

The Hike

Yosemite Falls is among the most famous and frequently photographed falls in the world and, according to some, is the highest on the continent at 2,425 feet. It is actually a series of three falls, the upper one dropping 1,430 feet, a middle series of cascades totaling 675 feet, and a lower one tumbling 320 feet; it qualifies as the highest only if all three are added together. In May and June the thunder of the water from melting snow falling onto the rocks below can be heard all over the Valley, and the spray drenches onlookers hundreds of feet away. On full-moon nights in May, visitors may see the famous "moonbow" first described by John Muir. The volume decreases as the summer wears on, and by September the falls are usually completely dry. In winter the frozen spray forms an eerie ice cone at the base.

From the picnic area the newly reconstructed trail winds almost imperceptibly uphill through ponderosa pine and incense cedar forest toward the base of the falls to a wide

Lower Yosemite Fall

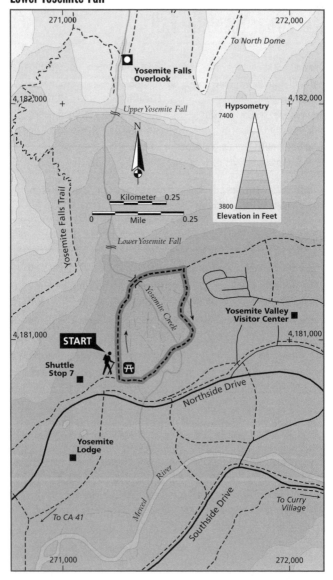

Yosemite Falls Overlook

To North Dome

Upper Yosemite Fall

N

Hypsometry

7400

3800

Elevation in Feet

0   Kilometer   0.25

0   Mile   0.25

Yosemite Falls Trail

Lower Yosemite Fall

Yosemite Creek

Yosemite Valley
Visitor Center

START

Shuttle
Stop 7

Northside Drive

Yosemite
Lodge

Merced River

To CA 41

Southside Drive

To Curry
Village

271,000
272,000
4,182,000
4,181,000

viewing area and a bridge. At several points along the route are turnouts with interpretive panels about the human and natural history of the area that are well worth pausing to read. The bridge crosses the creek very near the base of the cliff. If it is early spring, you're sure to be dampened by the spray. Despite posted warning signs, the huge slippery boulders are usually crawling with people. Beyond the bridge the trail follows along the base of the cliff, then swings south behind some of the park employee housing. It winds past braided strands of the now divided creek, curves again to parallel Northside Drive, then returns to the starting point at the picnic area.

Miles and Directions

0.0   Trailhead.

0.2   Cross the bridge at Lower Yosemite Fall.

0.6   Trailhead.

5 Bridalveil Fall

Type of hike: Out-and-back.
Total distance: 0.8 mile.
Elevation gain: 50 feet.
Topo map: USGS El Capitan.
Starting point: Bridalveil Fall parking lot.

Best time to go: Spring, summer, and fall. The trail is icy and dangerous in winter.
Facilities: Pit toilets are available.

Finding the trailhead: The parking lot is on the Wawona Road (Highway 41) about 1.5 miles after you emerge from the east portal of the Wawona tunnel, and before the road splits into Northside and Southside Drives, which are one-way roads. Watch carefully for the sign on the right (southeast). If you miss it, you'll have to drive all the way around the Valley to get back. You cannot approach the fall by car from the east. Unfortunately, the Valley shuttle bus doesn't come this far.

The Hike

Bridalveil Creek flows over the southern wall of Yosemite Valley through a defile between Cathedral Rocks and the Leaning Tower, but before it reaches the bottom, 620 feet below, the wind catches, tatters, and flings the droplets into graceful, lacy patterns.

Follow the trail signs up a wide, paved path to a sign at a fork at 0.1 mile. Climb the right (south) fork along the tumbling, boulder-strewn stream to the vista point near the base of the fall at 0.2 mile. In spring, when the fall is full, you are bound to get soaked from the spray. The flow diminishes in summer, and by autumn it is often no more than a trickle that disappears halfway down the cliff face. The wind shifts

Bridalveil Fall

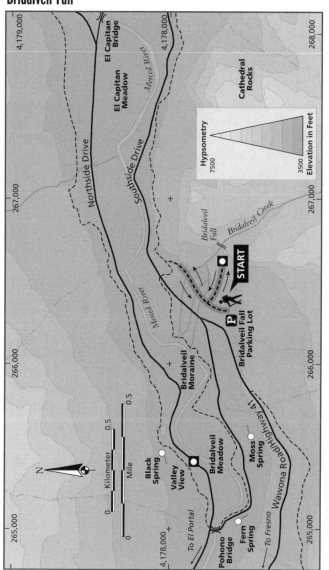

almost constantly, and the changing patterns of the falling water can be mesmerizing.

When you are ready, return to the trail junction at 0.3 mile, and for a different perspective take the left (north) fork for 0.1 mile, crossing three bridges over divided strands of the creek under an aromatic forest cover of bigleaf maple, bay tree, black oak, and incense cedar. Between the trees, at 0.4 mile, are framed views of the fall. Return to the parking lot the way you came.

Miles and Directions

0.0   Trailhead.

0.1   Reach a trail fork.

0.2   Arrive at the vista point.

0.3   Return to the trail fork.

0.4   Reach the lower viewpoint.

0.8   Trailhead.

6 Mariposa Grove

Type of hike: Out-and-back (with optional loops).
Total distance: 1.6 miles.
Elevation gain: 100 feet.
Maps: USGS Mariposa Grove; "Mariposa Grove of Giant Sequoias Guide and Map" by Jon Kinney, available at the trailhead for 50 cents.

Starting point: Mariposa Grove trailhead.
Best time to go: Spring, summer, or fall, or until snow closes the road.
Facilities: Restrooms, water, snacks, a telephone, and a gift shop are available near the parking lot.

Finding the trailhead: From the entrance station to Yosemite on the Wawona Road (Highway 41), head right (east) for 2 miles to the Mariposa Grove. There is limited parking at the trailhead, but you can park in the lot across the street from the entrance station and ride the free shuttle bus, or you can catch the bus in front of the store in Wawona. The buses run about every twenty minutes. A sign at the northeast end of the parking lot marks the trailhead.

The Hike

The giant sequoias are the largest living organisms on earth and, at up to 3,000 years old, are among the oldest. The bristlecone pines in the White Mountains to the east are older, and the coast redwoods are taller, but these are certainly the most massive and arguably the most awe-inspiring of the big trees. Yosemite has three groves of these trees; the Mariposa is the most popular, and the Grizzly Giant is the largest tree in all of them.

Mariposa Grove

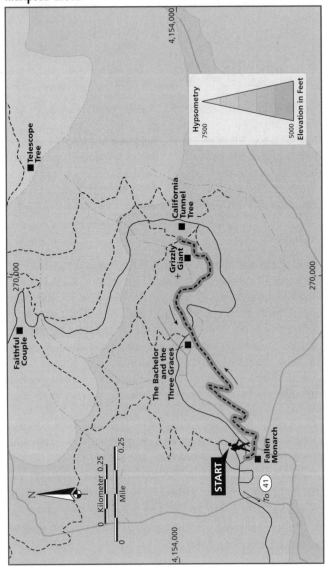

A narrated tram tour is available to those who prefer to ride. It uses the paved road that was built years ago when private cars were still allowed inside the grove. A veritable maze of well-marked footpaths runs through the grove, so you can design a pleasant hike of any length.

The route described here takes you to two of the most famous trees in the grove. The trail is marked by a series of interpretive panels with fascinating tidbits of information about the trees, among them the fact that these giants have very shallow root systems and very tiny seeds and that they depend upon fire to maintain their health and reproduction.

From the busy parking lot, follow the signed trail (and the crowds) eastward along the main trail to the Fallen Monarch at 0.1 mile, made famous by an old photograph of a group of soldiers—on horseback—posed along the top. Cross the tram road and climb gently to a beautiful grouping called the Bachelor and the Three Graces at 0.3 mile.

The path climbs a bit more steeply for the next 0.5 mile to the massive Grizzly Giant at 0.8 mile. According to park literature, a single one of its lower limbs is larger than the trunk of any non-sequoia here, and other authorities maintain that it is larger than any tree east of the Mississippi. It is nearly 3,000 years old.

About 50 feet beyond the Grizzly Giant is the California Tunnel Tree. The tunnel was cut in 1895 for stagecoaches full of tourists to drive through. Years ago motorists could drive their cars through another of the sequoias here, the Wawona Tunnel Tree, but eventually its roots weakened, and the tree fell under the weight of an exceptionally heavy snowfall in 1969. From the California Tunnel Tree, return to the trailhead the way you came.

Miles and Directions

0.0   Mariposa Grove trailhead.

0.1   Reach the Fallen Monarch.

0.3   Pass the Bachelor and the Three Graces.

0.8   Arrive at the Grizzly Giant.

1.6   Trailhead.

7   Wawona Meadow

Type of hike: Loop.
Total distance: 3.5 miles.
Elevation gain: 100 feet.
Topo map: USGS Wawona.
Starting point: Wawona Golf Course.

Best time to go: April through June for wildflowers, though the trail is open all year.
Facilities: Lodging, store, gas, phones, and restrooms are available at Wawona. There are pit toilets at the trailhead.

Finding the trailhead: Drive to the little village of Wawona on the Wawona Road (Highway 41). The Wawona Hotel is on the north side of the road, the Wawona Golf Course on the south. Just across from the hotel, Chowchilla Mountain Road cuts through the middle of the golf course. On the far side of the golf course, the parking area and trailhead are marked by a big signboard with photos and information about the area.

The Hike

Wildflower lovers will find some rare and unusual species blooming along the trail in Wawona Meadow in early season. Down among the grasses and sedges of the meadow, look for little three-petaled white star tulips in May. The tall

Wawona Meadow

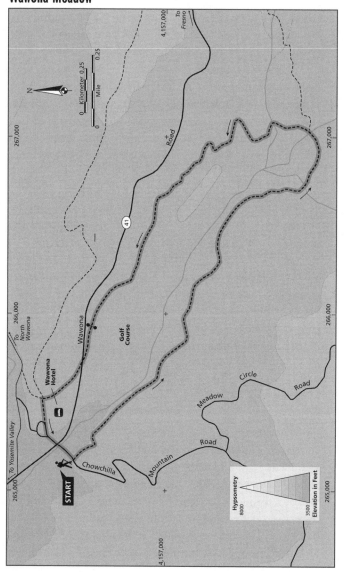

To Fresno

4,157,000

N

0   Kilometer 0.25

0   0.25
                    Mile

267,000

Road

267,000

41

To North
Wawona

266,000

Wawona

Wawona
Hotel

Golf
Course

266,000

Circle

Road

Meadow

To Yosemite Valley

265,000

Mountain

Road

START

Chowchilla

Hypsometry

8000

Elevation in Feet

3500

265,000

4,157,000

cabbagelike stalks growing in clumps are the poisonous corn lily. There are islands of willow and chokecherry, usually broadcasting bird song from warblers and blackbirds.

On the shady forest floor, watch for saprophytes—leafless plants that live on decaying material in the soil—such as the scarlet snow plant, the knobby brown spikes of pinedrops, and the odd little orchids called coral root. You can even find lady's slipper orchids in damp patches. In June great clumps of western azalea burst into bloom, along with several kinds of lilies.

You can follow the route in either direction, but it will be described counterclockwise here. It follows an old, mostly dirt road that is no longer used by vehicles except at the spots where it crosses the Wawona Road.

Start by skirting the south side of the golf course under a cover of incense cedar and ponderosa pine. Leave the manicured lawn behind as the meadow begins. The border zone between forest and meadow, called the ecotone, is usually among the richest in living organisms. You might see a cluster of mule deer; they are very tame, but do not attempt to pet or feed them. Mule deer in Yosemite cause more serious injuries to tourists than do bears.

Now and then a little spur trail leads out into the meadow. It can be boggy and muddy toward the center, and the vegetation is fragile—step with care. At 1.7 miles a trail alongside a little creek leads right (east) toward the park's south entrance. Continue along the road and step across another little rivulet. The road becomes partly eroded asphalt and runs through a section of forest in which the bases of the trees are slightly blackened from a management fire. Cross the Wawona Road at 3.2 miles, just beyond the closed gate. The trail continues on to the Wawona Hotel, where, at 3.4

miles, it crosses the road to the south and cuts back through the golf course to the trailhead.

Miles and Directions

0.0 Trailhead.
1.7 Cross the creek to the trail junction.
3.2 Reach the first crossing of Wawona Road.
3.4 Cross Wawona Road a second time.
3.5 Trailhead.

8 Chilnualna Fall

Type of hike: Out-and-back.
Total distance: 0.4 mile.
Elevation gain: 100 feet.
Topo map: USGS Wawona.
Starting point: North Wawona.

Best time to go: Spring, summer, or fall. The trail can be icy and dangerous in winter.
Facilities: There are none at the trailhead.

Finding the trailhead: From the Wawona Road (Highway 41) about 200 feet beyond Wawona, turn right (east) onto the Chilnualna Fall Road. Drive 2 miles, passing through the little village of North Wawona, to a signed parking area on the right (east).

The Hike

Chilnualna Creek seldom flows quietly, but rushes and crashes and roars almost constantly for most of its length. One of the most spectacular sections of falling water is just above the point where Chilnualna Creek passes beneath the Chilnualna Fall Road and flows into the Merced River. It is

Chilnualna Fall

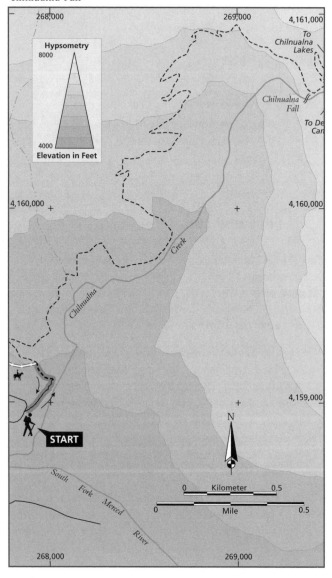

Hypsometry

8000

Elevation in Feet

4000

To Chilnualna Lakes

Chilnualna Fall

To De Car

Creek

Chilnualna

START

South Fork Merced River

| 0 | Kilometer | 0.5 |

| 0 | Mile | 0.5 |

N

as exciting as any of the more famous falls in Yosemite Valley, but few people see it, tucked away as it is in this little corner of the park. This trail takes you so close to the action that you're likely to get soaked from the spray if you go early in the year.

Follow the trail signs from the parking area and cross the road. A sign routes horse traffic to the left (north), hikers to the right (east). The footpath heads steeply up, sometimes on big granite steps right beside the thundering water. You go no more than 0.2 mile at creekside, but just standing next to all that power is exhilarating. Do not be tempted to continue scrambling up the slippery and treacherous rocks after the trail cuts left (west), away from the creek, but follow the trail to where it meets the horse trail that continues on up into the high country. You can return the way you came, but watch your step on the slick granite. If you prefer to make a loop, follow the horse trail back down along a paved road, past a few small vacation homes, to the parking area.

Miles and Directions

0.0 Trailhead.
0.2 Climb alongside the creek.
0.4 Trailhead.

Glacier Point Road Trails

⑨ Glacier Point

Type of hike: Out-and-back.
Total distance: 0.5 mile.
Elevation gain: Minimal.
Topo map: USGS Half Dome.
Starting point: Glacier Point parking lot.
Best time to go: Spring through fall. The Glacier Point Road is closed beyond the Badger Pass Ski Area in winter, but Glacier Point is a popular destination for experienced cross-country skiers.
Facilities: Food, water, telephones, and restrooms are available at the trailhead.

Finding the trailhead: From the junction at Chinquapin on the Wawona Road (Highway 41), drive up the Glacier Point Road about 16 miles to its end. You can also take a shuttle bus from Yosemite Valley to Glacier Point.

The Hike

The view from Glacier Point is surely one of the most spectacular in the world. Half Dome occupies center stage, brooding over slickrock Tenaya Canyon and Mirror Lake at the east end of Yosemite Valley. To the right the Merced River drops into the Valley over the Giant Staircase as Nevada and Vernal Falls. Rounded Mount Starr King and the darker-colored Clark Range lie beyond. Interpretive panels at the rim help you identify the distant peaks.

There will be no doubt about which way to go upon leaving the parking lot. Head toward Half Dome, which rears up out of the Valley to the north and is backed by granite peaks that stretch to the horizon. About 200 feet past the

Glacier Point

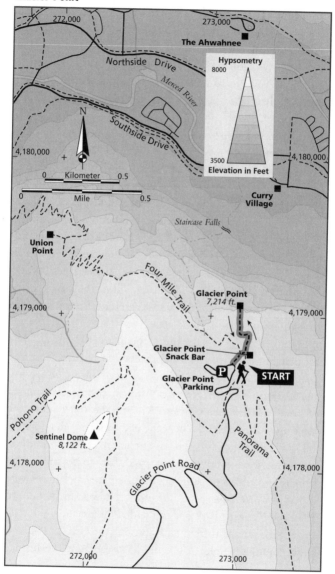

restrooms and the big area map, to the left (west) of the trail, is a snack bar and gift shop. To the right (southeast) there is an amphitheater for nighttime astronomy programs and an area from which hang gliders are launched early on summer mornings. You probably won't notice much of this, though, until you have absorbed the stupendous panoramas.

Turn left (west) along the path that passes below and in front of an old stone structure containing geologic exhibits about the formation of Yosemite Valley. Glacier Point itself lies slightly downhill and farther to the left (northwest) at 0.25 mile. It is a narrow overhanging platform 7,214 feet above sea level that is bound to look familiar even if this is your first trip to Yosemite. Among the famous photos taken here is that of a group of old-time cancan dancers in mid-kick. Peer over the railing at Curry Village and the remarkably flat bottom of Yosemite Valley 3,000 feet below, where the Merced River snakes from one end of the valley to the other. The double waterfall above Yosemite Lodge is 2,425-foot Yosemite Falls.

Until 1968 this was the site of the infamous "firefall." The bark of hundreds of the magnificent old red firs from the nearby forest was removed from the trees and set ablaze just after dark on summer evenings. After an elaborate ceremony of ritual calls between Glacier Point and the Valley below, the glowing coals were raked over the cliff to form a fiery waterfall in the dark. It was a popular attraction, of course, but one more suited to an amusement park than to Yosemite. The lichens and other organisms inhabiting the rock face were seared away, and the beautiful old forest was threatened. In 1968 the National Park Service ended the practice.

A park ranger is frequently on duty at Glacier Point to answer questions and give short lectures about the history and natural features of the area. Also on duty are innumerable obese, panhandling California ground squirrels. Please do not feed them; this will only encourage their delinquency and ill health.

Return to the trailhead as you came.

Miles and Directions

0.0 Trailhead.

0.25 Reach Glacier Point.

0.5 Trailhead.

10 Illilouette Fall

Type of hike: Out-and-back.
Total distance: 4.2 miles.
Elevation loss: 1,400 feet.
Topo map: USGS Half Dome.
Starting point: Glacier Point parking lot.
Best time to go: Spring and early summer. The hike back uphill can be hot and dusty later in the season.
Facilities: A snack bar, gift shop, water, restrooms, and telephones are available at Glacier Point. There are no facilities at Illilouette Fall.

Finding the trailhead: Follow the Glacier Point Road to its end 16 miles from Chinquapin on the Wawona Road (Highway 41), or take the shuttle from Yosemite Valley to Glacier Point. From the parking lot walk straight toward Half Dome, which looms up out of Yosemite Valley to the northeast. Near the rim of the cliff, turn right (east) on the worn path and go uphill to the big trailhead sign.

Illilouette Fall

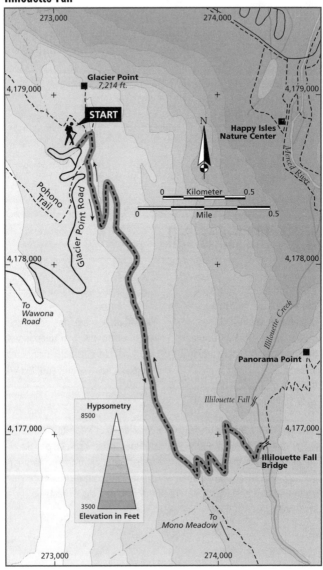

Glacier Point
7,214 ft.

START

N

Happy Isles
Nature Center

Merced River

Pohono
Trail

Glacier Point Road

Kilometer
0   0.5

Mile
0   0.5

To
Wawona
Road

Illilouette Creek

Panorama Point

Illilouette Fall

Hypsometry
8500

3500
Elevation in Feet

Illilouette Fall
Bridge

To
Mono Meadow

273,000   274,000

4,179,000

4,178,000

4,177,000

The Hike

This is an upside-down hike and should probably be considered at the very edge of "easy," but it isn't difficult if you take your time. Remember that it will take much longer to come back up from the fall than it did to go down. Make sure you have allowed plenty of time and that you carry water.

Before you begin take a minute to enjoy the overwhelming immensity of the panorama at the trailhead. To the left is North Dome, capping the graceful Royal Arches; in the center is Half Dome, the monumental symbol of Yosemite. Tenaya Canyon stretches away to the northeast, and to the west runs the Merced River canyon, down whose Giant Staircase flow Nevada and Vernal Falls. Beautifully sculpted Mount Clark and the Clark Range stretch off to the east.

The only confusing section of the whole route is at the beginning. Do not immediately strike out along the edge of the cliff to the left (north) of the trail sign, but head slightly uphill to the right (south). At 0.1 mile there are two more signs and two trails. To the right (west) is the Pohono Trail, which skirts Yosemite Valley to the west. The Panorama Trail, described here, goes left (south) toward Illilouette Fall.

The first mile of the trail switchbacks downward through an area burned in 1987. Fragrant ceanothus, and chinquapin with its spiny green fruits, line the path. This is a good place to listen for the booming call of the blue grouse in spring and early summer. Males find a territory to their liking, then sit and hoot, hour after hour, day after day, hoping to encourage a mate and discourage competitors. Their call is similar to the sound made when you blow across the mouth of a glass bottle.

At 1.2 miles a trail from Mono Meadow to the south joins the Illilouette Fall trail. Keep left (northeast) and continue to descend into the Illilouette Gorge. Shrubs give way to forest, and the rush of Illilouette Creek becomes audible. Other hikers have worn a little turnout to the left (north) of the trail to get a look at the fall, just out of sight from the trail itself. This is the only way to see most of Illilouette Fall from any direction, because it is tucked so tightly back into the gorge. Continue to descend a few more switchbacks to the footbridge over the creek. The fall is not visible from the footbridge, but the creek cascades down in picturesque wedding-cake fashion, and in springtime the blooms of western azaleas lining the banks perfume the air.

Return the way you came.

Miles and Directions

- **0.0** Start at the Panorama/Pohono trailheads.
- **0.1** Reach the Panorama/Pohono trail junction.
- **1.2** Pass the Mono Meadow trail junction.
- **2.1** Reach the Illilouette Fall bridge.
- **4.2** Panorama/Pohono trailheads.

11 Sentinel Dome

Type of hike: Out-and-back.
Total distance: 2.2 miles.
Elevation gain: 370 feet.
Topo map: USGS Half Dome.
Starting point: Sentinel Dome/Taft Point parking area.

Best time to go: Late spring through fall, as long as the Glacier Point Road is open.
Facilities: There is a pit toilet at the trailhead, but no water.

Finding the trailhead: From the Wawona Road (Highway 41) at Chinquapin, drive 13 miles east up the Glacier Point Road. Parking and the signed trailhead are on the left (northwest).

The Hike

The location of Sentinel Dome above Yosemite Valley provides complete 360-degree views of just about the whole park. Carry water and wear good sturdy shoes for this one; smooth-soled sandals won't give you enough traction.

This dome, like the others in Yosemite, owes its unique architecture to the nature of the rock itself. Though the movement of glaciers did not produce it, the scouring action of ice did polish and smooth the rough edges. Granitic rock forms when molten material under the earth's crust rises toward the surface but cools and solidifies before it gets there. As the surface material is eroded, pressure on the underlying granite is decreased and the rock expands. The kind of granitic rock that forms Sentinel Dome and others in Yosemite is so solid and massive that it does not break into pieces when it expands; instead, great sheets of rock pop loose, like layers of an onion, and erode.

The trail begins at a sign in a sandy opening in the forest that directs you to the right (northeast). The path to the

Sentinel Dome; Taft Point and the Fissures

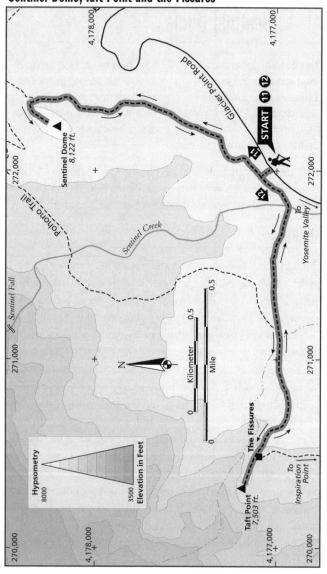

left (west) goes to Taft Point and the Fissures. The rough and rocky path crosses a brook, then undulates gradually upward, slowly revealing the top of the dome. Soon it curves to the left (north) and proceeds more steeply over smooth and featureless rock. Stenciled metal signs keep you on course.

At 0.4 mile a partly paved service road joins the trail from the right (east). Continue around the base of the dome on your left (west). When you have reached the "back" or more gradually sloping side of the dome at 0.6 mile, the Pohono Trail splits off to the right (north) and heads down to Glacier Point. Turn left (west) just beyond this point and head up the steep, open slope on a path of sorts. Don't worry if you lose the track; the only way to go is up. At the dome's summit are the remains of a gnarled Jeffrey pine, once the subject of innumerable photographs and postcards. It is dead now and has fallen but is still picturesque.

When you have caught your breath, make a slow circle around the summit. To the northwest the Yosemite Valley, flanked by the Cathedral Rocks on the left (south) and El Capitan on the right (north), stretches toward the coast. If the great Central Valley is free of smog (a rare occurrence), you can see all the way to the Coast Ranges. As you move clockwise to the northeast, the entire length of Yosemite Falls comes into view, and in early summer you can hear its roar from here. Farther east the Merced River canyon and Nevada Fall appear, then Mount Clark and the colorful Clark Range, providing a spiky backdrop for the rounded summit of Mount Starr King. The circle is closed by the lower forested country to the south.

When you are ready, descend very slowly and carefully, avoiding loose sand and gravel whenever possible, and return the way you came, taking care to follow the metal signs directing you to the parking lot.

Miles and Directions

0.0 Trailhead.

0.4 Reach the service road.

0.6 Pass the Pohono Trail to Glacier Point.

1.1 Reach the top of Sentinel Dome.

2.2 Trailhead.

12 Taft Point and the Fissures

See map on page 40

Type of hike: Out-and-back.
Total distance: 2.2 miles.
Elevation loss: 250 feet.
Topo map: USGS Half Dome.
Starting point: Glacier Point Road.
Best time to go: Spring, summer, or fall, as long as the Glacier Point Road is open.
Facilities: There is a pit toilet at the trailhead, but no water. Snacks and telephones are available at Glacier Point, 3 miles east down the road.

Finding the trailhead: From Chinquapin on the Wawona Road (Highway 41), turn east onto the Glacier Point Road and drive 13 miles to the parking area and signed trailhead, which is on the left (west) side.

The Hike

This is an upside-down excursion. After an easy cruise downhill to Taft Point, you will be climbing up on your way back. Be sure to give yourself plenty of time and to take water with you. Your reward is a striking set of geologic features that will help you understand how Yosemite got its famous profile, with a magnificent—and spine-tingling—view of Yosemite Valley as a bonus.

The trail begins at a sign in a sandy opening in the mixed pine and fir forest. Follow the path to the left (west). Sentinel Dome lies to the right (north). Pass through a flat, fairly open stretch past an odd, isolated outcrop of almost pure white quartz on the right (north), then swing left (south) and start downhill where the forest closes in. At 0.4 mile you reach the Pohono Trail junction and continue walking left (west). The trail sign here says you have come only 0.2 mile from the trailhead, but this is out-of-date and inaccurate. The forest deepens, and the little creek you will soon cross nourishes a colorful garden of moisture-loving cow parsnip, senecio, corn lily, knotweed, and shooting star. The trail emerges from the shady forest onto open rock and becomes steeper. The flower-filled gully on your right (north) abruptly narrows, deepens, and drops through a notch that sends the little creek plummeting toward the valley floor.

Descend carefully down the rocks past low patches of manzanita and the occasional Jeffrey pine. When the terrain begins to level out, watch for the Fissures on the right. They are narrow, deep cracks or joints in the granite, up to 40 feet long, slicing inward from the edge of the overhanging cliff, and are not visible until you are standing right at their edges. Peering over the side of the cliff, you can see that they cut completely through yards and yards of solid granite, below which there is nothing but close to 3,000 feet of thin air between you and the floor of Yosemite Valley. Because of the exposure, this is not a good choice for an evening hike in low light or for a walk with small, unrestrained children.

Once your internal butterflies have settled, proceed toward a slightly rising point with a protective iron railing around it that leans out over the Valley like the prow of a ship. This is Taft Point (1.1 miles). Directly across the Valley are the Three Brothers, produced by the same jointing process that opened the Fissures. To the left (west) is the vertical face of El Capitan; to the right (east) is Yosemite Falls. If you stroll westward along the rim, you can see the dramatic knife edges and needlelike spikes of Cathedral Spires.

When you are ready to return, descend the rise from Taft Point to the first trail sign. (There is a second sign beyond this one. Don't go that far.) The right-hand fork heads south along the Pohono Trail to Inspiration Point. The left (southeast) fork returns to the trailhead and parking area.

Miles and Directions

0.0 Trailhead.
0.4 Reach the Pohono Trail junction.
0.9 Pause at the Fissures.
1.1 Arrive at Taft Point.
2.2 Trailhead.

13 McGurk Meadow

Type of hike: Out-and-back.
Total distance: 1.6 miles.
Elevation loss: 60 feet.
Topo maps: USGS El Capitan and Half Dome.

Starting point: McGurk Meadow trailhead.
Best time to go: All summer, but the wildflowers are best in July.
Facilities: There are none at the trailhead.

Finding the trailhead: Drive about 8.5 miles up the Glacier Point Road from the junction with Highway 41 at Chinquapin. The trailhead is just before the entrance to the Bridalveil Creek Campground, but it's easy to miss. The campground is on the right (south) side of the road, and the trailhead is on the left (north). The easiest way to find it is to drive to the campground entrance, turn around, and head back (west) the way you came for about 200 yards. Park in the first turnout on the right. The trailhead sign is about 100 yards ahead, but there is nowhere to park near the sign.

The Hike

This is one of Yosemite's prettiest and "bloomingest" meadows. The path descends through a quiet lodgepole pine forest, and alongside the trail currants, strawberries, lupines, larkspur, and many other species flourish.

Just before you reach the meadow at 0.7 mile, watch for an old log cabin on the left (west). Beyond lies the meadow at 0.8 mile. It is threaded by a little brook and spangled with wildflowers of every color: shooting stars, lungwort, corn lily, monkeyflower, and paintbrush, to name a few.

The meadow is a fairly long one and the flower gardens continue for almost 2 miles, beyond which the McGurk Meadow trail meets the Pohono Trail. If you don't care to

McGurk Meadow

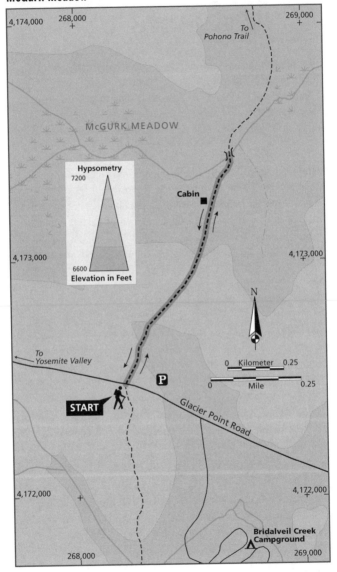

To Pohono Trail

McGURK MEADOW

Hypsometry

7200

6600

Elevation in Feet

Cabin

4,174,000
4,173,000
4,172,000

268,000
269,000

N

0   Kilometer   0.25

0   Mile   0.25

To Yosemite Valley

P

START

Glacier Point Road

Bridalveil Creek
Campground

venture so far into the meadow, you can find a pleasant spot near the footbridge to linger along its edges. Such a meeting of forest and meadow is one of the best places for wildlife watching during the morning and evening hours.

Retrace your steps to the trailhead.

Miles and Directions

0.0 Trailhead.

0.7 Pass the old log cabin.

0.8 Reach McGurk Meadow.

1.6 Trailhead.

Tioga Road Trails

14 Tuolumne Grove

Type of hike: Lollipop loop.
Total distance: 2.0 miles.
Elevation loss: 480 feet.
Topo map: USGS Ackerson Mountain.
Starting point: Tuolumne Grove trailhead.

Best time to go: Spring, summer, and fall, as long as the Tioga Road is open.
Facilities: There are toilets at the parking lot.

Finding the trailhead: From Yosemite Valley, drive 16 miles north on the Big Oak Flat Road (Highway 41) to Crane Flat. Turn right (east) on the Tioga Road (Highway 120) and drive less than a mile to the Tuolumne Grove parking area on the left (west).

The Hike

The Tuolumne Grove of giant sequoias is not as heavily visited as the Mariposa Grove, and because it does not have a tram tour through it, you can enjoy the beauty and serenity of the forest away from the sounds of "civilization."

The route follows an old road now closed to vehicle traffic. It passes through a closed gate and descends into a beautiful old forest of white fir, Douglas fir, sugar pine, and incense cedar. This last, with its distinctive red bark, is often confused with the giant sequoia, but the first of these will not appear for about 0.5 mile. In spring exquisite white dogwoods bloom in openings in the forest.

The first huge sequoia, with an interpretive panel beside it, appears on the left (west) at about 1.0 mile. A sign to the

Tuolumne Grove

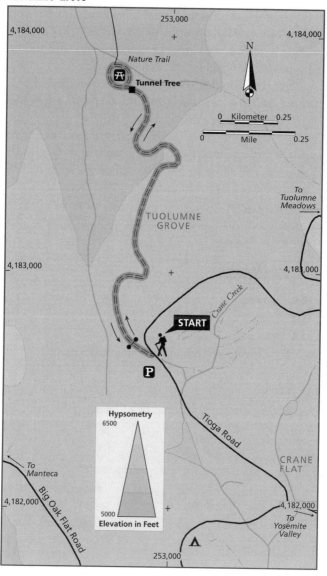

Nature Trail
Tunnel Tree

To Tuolumne Meadows

TUOLUMNE GROVE

Crane Creek

START

P

Tioga Road

CRANE FLAT

To Manteca

Big Oak Flat Road

To Yosemite Valley

N

| 0 | Kilometer | 0.25 |
| 0 | Mile | 0.25 |

Hypsometry

6500

5000

Elevation in Feet

4,184,000

4,183,000

4,182,000

253,000

right (north) directs you to the Tunnel Tree. This tree was already just a stump when the tunnel was cut through it in 1878, but dead or alive, the stump evokes an eerie feeling when you look straight up from the inside.

Beyond the Tunnel Tree is a picnic area that used to be a parking lot when cars were allowed through the grove. The nature trail begins here, on the right (northeast) and across a little bridge. It has a series of excellent interpretive signs explaining the natural history of the trees: how they reach their great ages of up to 3,000 years; how they adapted to survive repeated fires; how they depend on fires, insects, and squirrels to reproduce; and more. The nature trail loop returns to the road at the picnic area. Climb back up the road to the trailhead.

Miles and Directions

0.0 Trailhead.

1.0 Reach Tuolumne Grove.

2.0 Trailhead.

15 Lukens Lake

Type of hike: Out-and-back.
Total distance: 1.6 miles.
Elevation gain: 150 feet.
Topo map: USGS Yosemite Falls.
Starting point: Lukens Lake trailhead.

Best time to go: All summer, when the Tioga Road is open.
Facilities: There are none at the trailhead.

Finding the trailhead: Drive about 2 miles east of the White Wolf junction on the Tioga Road (Highway 120). The signed parking area is on the right (south) side of the road, but the trail begins on the left (north) side.

The Hike

To begin this hike, carefully cross the Tioga Road and head uphill through an almost pure red-fir forest. The cones underfoot come from the occasional western white pine or hemlock; fir cones do not fall, but decompose and release their seeds while still on the tree. Watch for odd, leafless plants like pinedrops, brilliant red snow plant, and little saprophytic orchids on the forest floor. Chinquapin, green and gold shrubs with spiny but delicious nuts, grow in the sunny spots.

The trail tops a rise, then descends to a creek filled with dozens of species of waist-high wildflowers. This display makes Lukens Lake a favorite of wildflower lovers. The trail turns left (northwest) at 0.7 mile and follows the creek to Lukens Lake. The moisture that allows for the lushness of the wildflowers means lots of mosquitoes. Take repellent.

Retrace your steps to the Tioga Road.

Lukens Lake

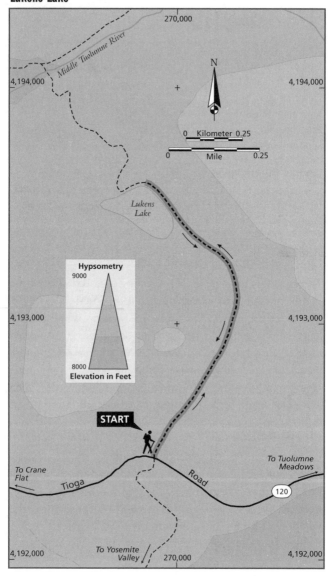

Miles and Directions

0.0 Trailhead.

0.7 Reach and follow the creek.

0.8 Arrive at Lukens Lake.

1.6 Trailhead.

16 May Lake

Type of hike: Out-and-back.
Total distance: 2.4 miles.
Elevation gain: 500 feet.
Topo map: USGS Tenaya Lake.
Starting point: May Lake trailhead.
Best time to go: All summer, as long as the Tioga Road is open and free of snow.

Facilities: Toilets and water are available at May Lake. Please use the toilets at the campground, not at the High Sierra Camp. There is also a small store at the High Sierra Camp that is open for a few hours each day. There are no facilities at the trailhead.

Finding the trailhead: The May Lake road junction lies along the Tioga Road (Highway 120) 27 miles east of Crane Flat and 20 miles west of Tioga Pass. Follow the narrow road north about 2 miles to the trailhead. Drive with care. In many places the road is wide enough for only one vehicle. Leave any food or ice chests in the bear-proof boxes at the trailhead.

The Hike

The hike begins in a shady glen with a variety of conifers—lodgepole, silver pine, hemlock, and fir—and passes a little brown pond teeming with fairy shrimp and other interesting creatures. The well-used trail climbs slowly at first, passing

May Lake

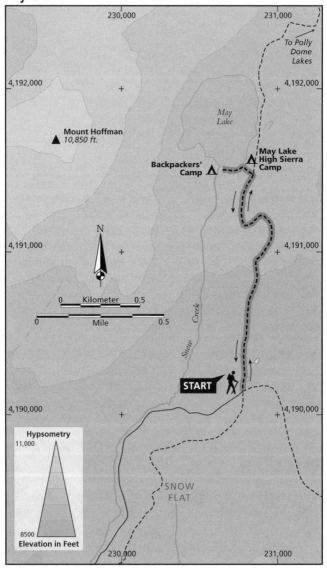

To Polly Dome Lakes

May Lake

Mount Hoffman
10,850 ft.

Backpackers' Camp

May Lake High Sierra Camp

N

0   Kilometer   0.5

0   Mile   0.5

Snow Creek

START

SNOW FLAT

Hypsometry
11,000

8500
Elevation in Feet

through granite corridors where cracks bloom with ferns, mountain's pride penstemon, shaggy hawkweed, and other wildflowers. The trail ascends gradually, then begins a steeper, winding climb. There are good views now and then down Tenaya Canyon to the left (southwest), past Clouds Rest and Half Dome. The dramatic pointy peak in the distance is Mount Clark. Back up the canyon to the right (southeast), you can just glimpse Tenaya Lake.

The trail flattens out in forest and reaches a trail fork at May Lake at 1.2 miles. To the left (west) is the camping area; to the right (east) is the High Sierra Camp, one of five popular backcountry camps with tent cabins and other amenities that are available to park visitors by reservation only. If you don't count Tuolumne Meadows Lodge, this camp is the most easily reached.

Enjoy the lakeshore, but do not jump in. This is the local water supply, and swimming is prohibited. Mount Hoffman, at 10,850 feet, rises dramatically behind the lake to the west.

Miles and Directions

0.0 Trailhead.
1.2 Reach May Lake.
2.4 Trailhead.

17 Olmstead Point Nature Trail

Type of hike: Out-and-back.
Total distance: 0.6 mile.
Elevation gain: 300 feet.
Topo map: USGS Tenaya Lake.
Starting point: Olmstead Point parking area.

Best time to go: All summer, as long as the Tioga Road is open and the trails are free of ice.
Facilities: There are none.

Finding the trailhead: Drive about 9 miles west of the Tuolumne Meadows Visitor Center on the Tioga Road (Highway 120). Watch for the signed parking area on the south side of the road, a little more than 1 mile southwest of Tenaya Lake.

The Hike

Most visitors hop out of their cars at Olmstead Point, take a snapshot of the view, then drive away. By descending only a very short distance from the parking lot, however, you will be rewarded with a true sense of the majesty of Yosemite. The stupendous gorge of Tenaya Canyon yawns all around you. You can feel the wind in the rocks, smell the conifers and the wildflowers, hear the chuckling of grouse and the whistle of marmots. To the south the exfoliating granite of Clouds Rest forms intricate patterns. Half Dome lies beyond. Behind you to the north is Tenaya Lake, deep, deep blue in its basin of ice-polished granite.

Begin at the interpretive panel explaining the formation of Yosemite's domes, and proceed downhill along a rock-lined path to a trail junction. The right (west) fork goes down to Yosemite Valley, while the left (northeast) skirts the Tioga Road heading to Tenaya Lake. Follow the trail straight

18 Tenaya Lake

Type of hike: Out-and-back or 1.5-mile shuttle.
Total distance: 3.0 miles.
Elevation gain: Negligible.
Topo map: USGS Tenaya Lake.
Starting point: The picnic area parking lot at the northeast end of Tenaya Lake.
Best time to go: All summer, when the Tioga Road is open.
Facilities: There are toilets at the trailhead.

Finding the trailhead: Ride the free shuttle bus from Tuolumne Meadows to stop 9 at the northeast end of Tenaya Lake or drive to the same spot on the Tioga Road (Highway 120). Turn southeast into the picnic area parking lot, where you will find toilets, bear boxes, and a sign directing you to the trail. There is another picnic area about halfway along the length of the lake just off the Tioga Road, but the trail begins in the one at the northeast end of the lake.

The Hike

Tenaya Lake was named for Chief Tenaya, who, with all his people, was driven from his home in Yosemite by the U.S. Cavalry. It is a very big lake by Yosemite standards and a very popular one, too, with its wide sandy beach and its proximity to the road.

Follow the trail sign to the picnic tables on the beach and head south along the shore. Unless it is quite late in the summer, you will probably have to wade the inlet creek at 0.2 mile. The beach is a good vantage point from which to watch climbers clinging to the bare rock faces of the surrounding domes.

Pick up the obvious trail that runs alongside the lake's south shore. Stroll through garden after garden of wildflowers

Tenaya Lake

START

P

Tenaya Creek

To Tuolumne Meadows

Tioga Road

Murphy Creek

Tenaya Lake

120

To Yosemite Valley

Tenaya Creek

N

Hypsometry

Elevation in Feet

9600

8000

0   0.25   Kilometer

0   0.25   Mile

4,190,000

284,000

283,000

4,190,000

beside several trickling brooks, and wander as far as you wish along the lakeside before returning to the trailhead.

If you don't want to retrace your steps, hike 1.5 miles to the Sunrise Lakes trailhead at the west end of the lake. Turn right (west) and follow the Sunrise Lakes Trail a short distance to the Tioga Road at shuttle stop 10. Ride the shuttle back to stop 9. You can circumnavigate the entire lake, but once you reach its north side, you must walk on the shoulder of the busy Tioga Road for the whole length of the lake to get back to the parking lot.

Miles and Directions

0.0 Trailhead.

0.2 Cross the inlet creek.

1.5 Reach the Sunrise Lakes Trail.

3.0 Return to trailhead.

Tuolumne Meadows Trails

19 Pothole Dome

Type of hike: Out-and-back.
Total distance: 1.0 mile.
Elevation gain: 200 feet.
Topo map: USGS Falls Ridge.
Starting point: Pothole Dome parking area.

Best time to go: All summer, as long as the Tioga Road is open.
Facilities: There are none at the trailhead.

Finding the trailhead: Following the Tioga Road (Highway 120), drive or ride the Tuolumne Meadows shuttle about 1.5 miles west of the visitor center. The parking area and trailhead are on the right (north) side of the road. There are several signs, including an interpretive panel about life in the meadow.

The Hike

Pothole Dome looks like a much smaller version of Lembert Dome and is located at the west end of Tuolumne Meadows. It is such a popular hike that the vegetation between the road and the dome is in danger of becoming trampled—please stay on the trail.

The trail skirts the meadow to the west and crosses over to the dome along the edge of the forest, then swings right (east), back toward the low end of the dome, forming a wide U. Skirt the edge of the dome until you reach a convenient place to start up the long smooth slope to its summit.

Here you will find a number of fine examples of glacial activity. There are patches of glacial polish, rock surfaces

Pothole Dome

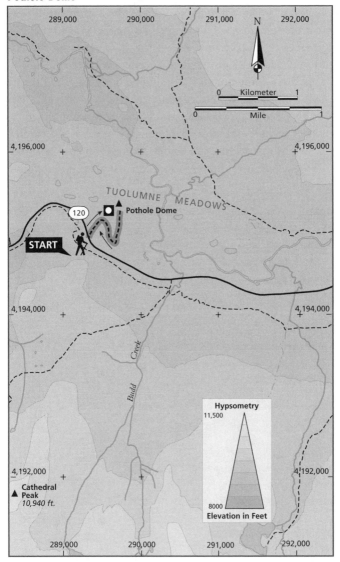

buffed to an almost blinding sheen by the movement of fine grit dragged across the rock by moving ice. Huge boulders improbably perched on top of the dome were deposited there by the glaciers. Here and there are the potholes for which the dome was named, hollowed out by swirling water trapped beneath the glacial ice.

Enjoy the spectacular 360-degree view from the top, which includes the northern boundary of the park; Mount Gibbs, Mount Dana, and Lembert Dome to the east; and the Cathedral Range to the south. Return, slowly and carefully, to the trailhead using the same trail.

Miles and Directions

- **0.0** Trailhead.
- **0.5** Reach the summit of Pothole Dome.
- **1.0** Trailhead.

20 Dog Lake

Type of hike: Out-and-back.
Total distance: 3.2 miles.
Elevation gain: 600 feet.
Topo map: USGS Tioga Pass.
Starting point: Lembert Dome parking lot.
Best time to go: Late spring to fall, when the Tioga Road is open.

Facilities: There are picnic tables and toilets at the trailhead, but no potable water. Supplies, a telephone, and groceries are available at the Tuolumne Meadows store, which is about 0.5 mile west on the Tioga Road.

Finding the trailhead: From the west drive the Tioga Road (Highway 120) eastward past the Tuolumne Meadows Visitor Center, store, and campground, all on the right (south) side of the road. About 150 yards beyond the bridge over the Tuolumne River, turn left (north) into the Lembert Dome parking area. From the east (Tioga Pass), follow the Tioga Road past the turnoff to the Wilderness Center on the left (south). The sign for the center reads WILDERNESS PERMITS, PACIFIC CREST, JOHN MUIR. About 100 yards beyond the sign, turn right (north) into the Lembert Dome lot.

The Hike

Set out northward from the Lembert Dome/Dog Lake trailhead sign through lodgepole pines. Cross an open rocky slab polished to a high sheen in places by glaciers, then reenter the forest. At 0.2 mile a trail comes in from the stables to the left (west). Take the right (north) fork. Just beyond, another trail comes in from the stables. Keep right (north) again. Climb steeply alongside the sheer face of Lembert Dome, then cross a little creek. The grade becomes less extreme.

Dog Lake

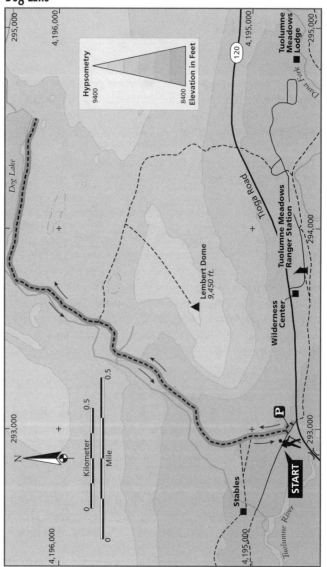

At 1.1 miles a trail cuts off to the right (east) around the back of Lembert Dome. Continue straight (north) toward Dog Lake. At 1.5 miles turn right (east) onto the Dog Lake Trail, and at 1.6 miles reach an opening in the forest that frames the lake perfectly. The sign at the lake says the water level is 9,240 feet, but it is marked 9,170 feet on the USGS topographic map. Take your pick.

Dog Lake is surrounded on three sides by lodgepole pines, but at the far east end, a green (or golden, depending on the season) meadow provides the foreground for the huge red bulks of Mount Dana and Mount Gibbs. Camping is not permitted here; tempting as it may be, the area is too delicate and too close to the busy road and would be trampled in no time. If you have decided not to walk all the way around the lake, return the way you came.

Miles and Directions

0.0 Trailhead.

0.2 Pass the trails from the stables.

1.1 A trail goes east to Lembert Dome.

1.5 Reach the Dog Lake cutoff.

1.6 Arrive at Dog Lake.

3.2 Trailhead.

Option: The official, mapped trail continues for about 0.5 mile along the south shore of the lake, but it is possible to circumambulate the lake, adding about 1.5 miles to your hike. The meadow around the lakeshore, especially at the east and north ends, can be boggy and wet and is very fragile—travel with care. At the northeast end of the lake, you will have a good view of Cathedral Peak poking up through the forest.

21 Lembert Dome

Type of hike: Loop.
Total distance: 3.1 miles.
Elevation gain: 500 feet.
Topo map: USGS Tioga Pass.
Starting point: Lembert Dome parking lot.
Best time to go: Late June through mid-September, as long as the Tioga Road is open.

Facilities: There are picnic tables and restrooms at the trailhead. Groceries, a telephone, and supplies can be found 0.5 mile to the west at the Tuolumne Meadows store.

Finding the trailhead: From the west follow the Tioga Road (Highway 120) past the Tuolumne Meadows Visitor Center, store, cafe, and campground, all on the right (south) side of the road. About 150 yards beyond the bridge over the Tuolumne River, turn left (north) into the Lembert Dome parking area. From the east (Tioga Pass), follow the Tioga Road past the turnoff to the Wilderness Center on the left (south) side of the road. Continue for about 100 yards, then turn right (north) into the Lembert Dome parking area.

The Hike

Lembert Dome, among the premier features of Tuolumne Meadows, is the huge, lopsided, smoothly polished mound of granite just north of the Tioga Road. This loop will take you all the way around the dome, providing some great views along the way. There are even better views from the top, of course, but the route is strenuous and slippery and far beyond the definition of an "easy" hike. You can follow the route in either direction, but it will be described clockwise here.

Set out northward, past the picnic tables and restrooms near the Lembert Dome/Dog Lake trailhead sign. Pass beneath lodgepole pines, then cross an open rocky slab

Lembert Dome

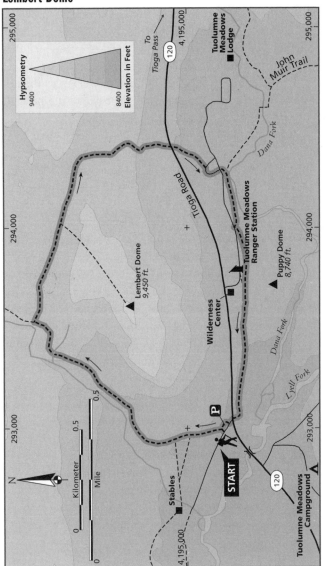

where the route is marked by big boulders. The granite is polished to a high sheen in patches by glaciers. If you look carefully, you can see striations, or scratches, in the rock that show the direction in which the rivers of ice flowed.

At 0.2 mile a trail comes in from the stables to the left (west). Take the right (north) fork. Just beyond, another trail comes in from the same direction. Keep right (north) again.

Climb alongside the sheer face of Lembert Dome, then cross a little creek. The grade becomes more gradual. At 1.1 miles, turn right (east) at the signed junction. The left fork goes north and uphill to Dog Lake. Saunter along an almost flat path, passing a little pond at the base of the dome. At 1.7 miles, you will reach another trail junction not shown on the topo; this one leads to the top of Lembert Dome. Your trail continues downhill to the left (south). Follow the steep switchbacks downhill to the Tioga Road. Cross the road at 2.5 miles, and continue 0.1 mile to a parking lot on a small side road that leads to Tuolumne Meadows Lodge. Cross the road to the south and find a trail sign marking the John Muir Trail at 2.6 miles. Turn right (west) and follow the John Muir Trail alongside the Tioga Road to where you can cross the road into the Lembert Dome parking area.

Miles and Directions

0.0   Trailhead.
0.2   Pass the trails from the stables.
1.1   Reach the Lembert Dome/Dog Lake trail junction.
1.7   Pass the trail to the top of the dome.
2.5   Cross the Tioga Road.
2.6   Pass the John Muir Trail sign.
3.1   Trailhead.

Option: If you decide to go to the summit of Lembert Dome, turn right at the trail intersection at 1.7 miles. You will add 0.6 mile and 350 feet of elevation gain to your hike.

22 Soda Springs and Parsons Lodge

Type of hike: Out-and-back.
Total distance: 1.2 miles.
Elevation gain: 40 feet.
Topo maps: USGS Tioga Pass and Vogelsang Peak.
Starting point: Tioga Road in Tuolumne Meadows.

Best time to go: All summer, as long as the Tioga Road is open.
Facilities: Food, water, gas, a post office, and telephones are all available nearby in Tuolumne Meadows village.

Finding the trailhead: From the visitor center in Tuolumne Meadows, drive about 150 yards east on the Tioga Road (Highway 120) to the signed trailhead on the left (north) side of the road.

The Hike

A wide, sandy trail heads right into the heart of enormous Tuolumne Meadows amid a riot of wildflowers: purple meadow penstemon, shooting stars, white pussytoes, and yellow goldenrod. The Tuolumne River winds its sinuous way through the meadow. Off to the right (east) is long, sloping Lembert Dome, and beyond, the two red bulks of Mounts Dana and Gibbs. To their right (south) is gray granite Mammoth Peak.

At the main channel of the river, the path crosses a wood and stone footbridge. Pause here and turn around for a panoramic view of the Cathedral Range to the south. The spires of Cathedral Peak itself, along with Echo Peak and the

Soda Springs and Parsons Lodge

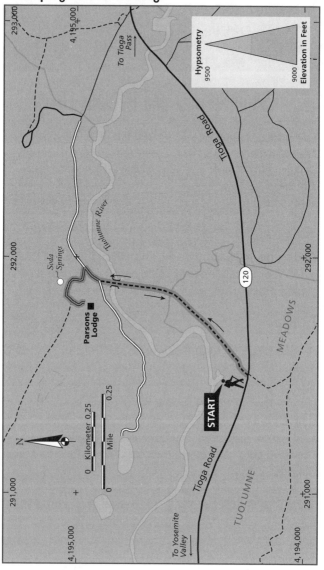

Cockscomb, rise behind smoothly rounded Fairview Dome.

About 10 feet beyond the bridge, the trail intersects a gravel road at 0.4 mile. Turn left (west) here and proceed about 50 yards to a sign directing you right (north) and up a little slope to Soda Springs and Parsons Lodge (0.6 mile).

Parsons Lodge, built of local stone by the Sierra Club in 1915 and sold to the National Park Service in 1973, is open daily during the summer and contains exhibits about the history of the area. Next door, the log-built McCauley Cabin houses National Park Service volunteers who are eager to share information about the area. Rest for a while on the rocks in front of the lodge to watch the activities of the marmot families that live in nearby burrows.

From the lodge head toward the tumbledown, roofless log structure clearly visible to the east. Here, naturally carbonated Soda Springs bubbles out of the ground in dozens of places, staining the soil red-brown. It's a good place to see mule deer, which come to lick the minerals deposited by the springs. You can spend a whole day wandering these meadows, using the well-marked trails to create your own loop, or you can return the way you came to the Tioga Road.

Miles and Directions

0.0   Trailhead.
0.4   Reach the gravel road.
0.6   Arrive at Parsons Lodge.
1.2   Trailhead.

23 Lyell Fork

Type of hike: Out-and-back.
Total distance: 1.2 miles.
Elevation gain: 60 feet.
Topo maps: USGS Tioga Pass and Vogelsang Peak.
Starting point: Dog Lake parking area.

Best time to go: All summer, as long as the Tioga Road is open.
Facilities: There are none at the trailhead, but food, phones, gas, water, and restrooms can all be found about 0.5 mile west on the Tioga Road at the Tuolumne Meadows store.

Finding the trailhead: From the west drive the Tioga Road (Highway 120) eastward past the Tuolumne Meadows Visitor Center, store, and campground, all on the right (south) side of the road. Cross the bridge over the Tuolumne River. About 0.5 mile beyond the bridge, turn right (south) at the entrance to the Wilderness Center and follow the road as it curves left (east) for 0.5 mile to the Dog Lake parking lot on the left (north). Store any food or ice chests in the bear-proof boxes provided. Do not leave anything that looks or smells like food in your car or trunk.

The Hike

This route is part of the famous John Muir Trail and the Pacific Crest Trail. Cross the road south of the parking lot to the trailhead sign. The trail rambles alongside the Dana Fork of the Tuolumne River before crossing it on a footbridge at 0.2 mile. Ignore the sign that points north to the Tuolumne Meadows Lodge. Turn left (east) just after the crossing. The trail continues along the Dana Fork before swinging south to the junction with the Gaylor Lakes Trail at 0.3 mile. Keep right (south), then pass a marshy area on the left (east), cross

Lyell Fork

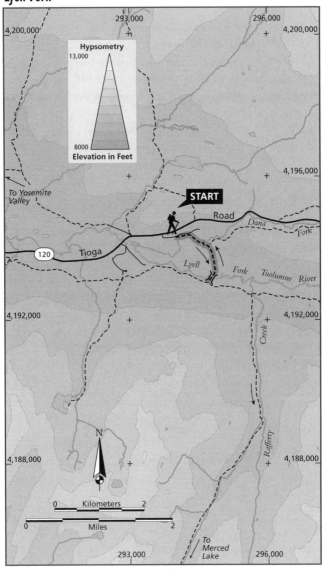

a low rocky rise, and turn right (south) to the two bridges over the Lyell Fork of the Tuolumne River.

The scene from the bridges must be one of the most sublime in Yosemite. The river is a brilliant turquoise ribbon winding through the long, green meadow. The massive gray hulk on the left (southeast) is Mammoth Peak (not to be confused with Mammoth Mountain, the ski resort, which lies further south). Where the river reaches the bridges it rushes over smoothly rounded rocks, swirling in beautiful patterns that have hollowed out perfectly round shallow bowls in the granite before tumbling into clear pools.

When you can tear yourself away, retrace your steps to the trailhead.

Miles and Directions

0.0 Dog Lake trailhead.

0.2 Cross the bridge over Dana Fork and pass the junction with the Tuolumne Meadows Lodge trail.

0.3 Reach the junction with the Gaylor Lakes Trail.

0.6 Arrive at the twin bridges over the Lyell Fork.

1.2 Trailhead.

Hetch Hetchy Trail

24 Wapama Falls

Type of hike: Out-and-back.
Total distance: 5.0 miles.
Elevation gain: 200 feet.
Topo map: USGS Lake Eleanor.
Starting point: O'Shaughnessy Dam parking area.
Best time to go: Mid-April to June. It's hot and dry later in the summer.

Facilities: You will find water, restrooms, and a telephone on the right side of the one-way loop road about 200 yards before you reach the dam and parking area.

Finding the trailhead: Drive 1 mile west of the Big Oak Flat Entrance Station to Yosemite National Park on Highway 120. Turn right (north) on Evergreen Road and drive about 7 miles. At Camp Mather turn right (northeast) on Hetch Hetchy Road. Pass through the park entrance station after about 1 mile, then continue for 8 miles to where the road ends in a one-way loop. Drive around the loop to the O'Shaughnessy Dam and parking area.

The Hike

Hetch Hetchy Reservoir, begun in 1914, completed in 1923, then expanded in 1938, provides water and power for the City of San Francisco; no swimming or boating is allowed. Before the dam captured and tamed the Tuolumne River, the Hetch Hetchy Valley was said to rival Yosemite in scenic beauty. John Muir's famous, if fruitless, battle against the dam brought the need to preserve such wilderness treasures to the attention of the public and gave impetus to the growth of the National Park Service and to the conservation movement as a whole. Even now a campaign is under way

Wapama Falls

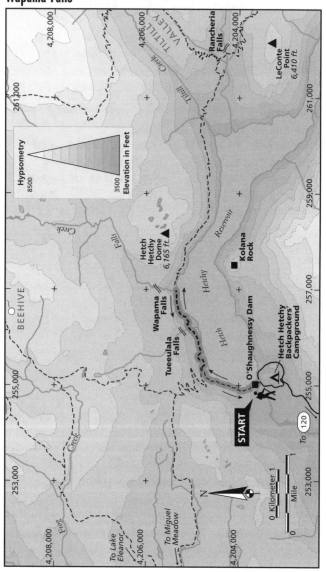

to convince legislators to raze the dam, drain the reservoir, and allow Hetch Hetchy to return to its original state.

The area around the lake has the best springtime wild-flowers in the park, and it's a good place to go in early season when the higher country is still under snow.

To begin, walk across the dam, past some historical markers. On the far side, at 0.1 mile, enjoy the troupe of acrobatic swallows swooping and diving before the entrance to a dark and dripping tunnel. Pass through the tunnel and continue along the level road skirting the lake.

The roadside is lined with live oak, bay trees, and poison oak, along with dozens of species of wildflowers. The low elevation here makes this a likely spot for encounters with snakes of several kinds, including rattlers. They are not aggressive, but should be avoided. If you're lucky, you'll catch the spring migration of millions of little brown-and-orange California newts. In the sunny places by the trail grow beautiful and unusual pink-and-yellow harlequin lupines. Water trickles down cracks in the rock and nourishes buttercups, monkeyflowers, columbines, and many other species.

The road climbs slowly for a while, then at 0.9 mile the trail to the falls leaves the road and turns right (east). The left (north) route leads to Lake Vernon. The Wapama Falls Trail rises and falls and curves back and forth past more delicate little gardens, waterfalls, and pools. Kolana Rock broods darkly over the reservoir on the other side.

Tueeulala Falls tumbles down over the trail. Early in the season you'll probably get your feet wet as you pass, but by June the little fall is usually dry. The trail continues along the cliff above the lake, climbing and descending, for 2.5 miles, until the spray and thunder of Wapama Falls make themselves felt. Toward the bottom the falls split into several sections, each of which is crossed on a separate footbridge. Sometimes the bridges are shin-deep under water, though safe to wade; at other times the force of the falling torrent is so great that it is not safe to cross. You can enjoy the falls from either side or from the middle if you crave a refreshing shower.

Return the way you came.

Miles and Directions

- **0.0** Hetch Hetchy trailhead.
- **0.1** Pass through the tunnel.
- **0.9** Reach the Lake Vernon trail junction.
- **2.5** Arrive at Wapama Falls.
- **5.0** Trailhead.

About the Author

Suzanne Swedo has taught natural science seminars for the Yosemite Association in Yosemite National Park for twenty years. During the same period she has conducted wilderness survival, outdoor skills, and natural history outings as founder and director of W.I.L.D., an international and domestic adventure travel company. She has also led nature and wilderness trips for various educational organizations including the University of California Extension, the National Outings Program of the Sierra Club, Wilderness Institute, Pacific Wilderness Institute, and Outdoor Adventures. She has demonstrated wilderness skills in a ten-week television series *Alive and Well* and served as a survival consultant for Warner Brothers Television. Her writings on travel and the outdoors have appeared in publications such as the *Los Angeles Examiner* and *California Magazine*. Other books for Falcon are *Wilderness Survival, Hiking California's Golden Trout Wilderness,* and *Hiking Yosemite*.

*Q*uality
guidebooks
for every
outdoor adventure.

best
easy
day hikes
Cape Cod

Cheryl Johnson Huban

Wilderness
First Aid

When
You Can't
Call 911

Gilbert Preston, M.D.
A FALCONGUIDE

A FALCONGUIDE
David Crowell
SECOND EDITION
**Mountain Biking
Moab
Pocket Guide**
42 of the Area's Greatest Off-Road Bicycle Rides

A FALCONGUIDE   Mountain Biking **Utah**
A FALCONGUIDE   Rock Climbing **New England**
A FALCONGUIDE   Hiking **Montana**
A FALCONGUIDE   Paddling **Minnesota**
A FALCONGUIDE   Scenic Byways **East & South**
A FALCONGUIDE   Fishing **Georgia**

A FALCONGUIDE
Dolores Kong and Dan Ring

Hiking
Acadia National Park

www.falcon.com